Davidson 304

POP ROCK

Popular Rock Superstars of Yesterday and Today

AC/DC	Elton John
Aerosmith	The Grateful Dead
The Allman Brothers Band	Led Zeppelin
The Beatles	Lynyrd Skynyrd
Billy Joel	Pink Floyd
Bob Marley and the Wailers	Queen
Bruce Springsteen	The Rolling Stones
The Doors	U2
	The Who

U2

Kenneth McIntosh

Mason Crest Publishers

U2

FRONTIS Few groups can claim the success that U2 has achieved—as musicians and as humanitarians in service to the world.

Produced by 21st Century Publishing and Communications, Inc.

Editorial by Harding House Publishing Services, Inc.

MASON CREST PUBLISHERS INC.
370 Reed Road
Broomall, Pennsylvania 19008
(866) MCP-BOOK (toll free)
www.masoncrest.com

Printed in the United States.

First Printing

9 8 7 6 5 4 3 2 1

Library of Congress Cataloging-in-Publication Data

McIntosh, Kenneth, 1959–
   U2 / Kenneth McIntosh.
     p. cm. — (Popular rock superstars of yesterday and today)
   Includes bibliographical references and index.
   Hardback edition: ISBN-13: 978-1-4222-0195-4
   Paperback edition: ISBN-13: 978-1-4222-0322-4
 1. U2 (Musical group)—Juvenile literature. 2. Rock musicians—Biography—
Juvenile literature. I. Title.
ML3930.U2M35 2008
782.42166092'2—dc22
[B]   2007012144

Publisher's notes:
- All quotations in this book come from original sources, and contain the spelling and grammatical inconsistencies of the original text.

- The Web sites mentioned in this book were active at the time of publication. The publisher is not responsible for Web sites that have changed their addresses or discontinued operation since the date of publication. The publisher will review and update the Web site addresses each time the book is reprinted.

CONTENTS

ROCK 'N' ROLL TIMELINE

1951
"Rocket 88," considered by many to be the first rock single, is released by Ike Turner.

1952
DJ Alan Freed coins and popularizes the term "Rock and Roll," proclaimes himself the "Father of Rock and Roll," and declares, "Rock and Roll is a river of music that has absorbed many streams: rhythm and blues, jazz, rag time, cowboy songs, country songs, folk songs. All have contributed to the Big Beat."

1955
"Rock Around the Clock" by Bill Haley & His Comets is released; it tops the U.S. charts and becomes wildly popular in Britain, Australia, and Germany.

1967
The Monterey Pop Festival in California kicks off open air rock concerts.

1965
The psychedelic rock band, the Grateful Dead, is formed in San Francisco.

1969
The Woodstock Music and Arts Festival attracts a huge crowd to rural upstate New York.

1969
Tommy, the first rock opera, is released by British rock band The Who.

1970
The Beatles break up.

1971
Jim Morrison, lead singer of The Doors, dies in Paris.

1971
Duane Allman, lead guitarist of the Allman Brothers Band, dies.

1950s   1960s   1970s

1957
Bill Haley tours Europe.

1957
Jerry Lee Lewis and Buddy Holly become the first rock musicians to tour Australia.

1954
Elvis Presley releases the extremely popular single "That's All Right (Mama)."

1961
The first Grammy for Best Rock 'n' Roll Recording is awarded to Chubby Checker for *Let's Twist Again*.

1964
The Beatles make their first visit to America, setting off the British Invasion.

1969
A rock concert held at Altamont Speedway in California is marred by violence.

1969
The Rolling Stones tour America as "The Greatest Rock and Roll Band in the World."

1973
Rolling Stone magazine names Annie Leibovitz chief photographer and "rock 'n' roll photographer;" she follows and photographs rockers Mick Jagger, John Lennon, and others.

1974
Sheer Heart Attack by the British rock band Queen becomes an international success.

1974
"Sweet Home Alabama" by Southern rock band Lynyrd Skynyrd is released and becomes an American anthem.

1987
Billy Joel becomes the first American rock star to perform in the Soviet Union since the construction of the Berlin Wall.

2005
Led Zeppelin is ranked #1 on VH1's list of the 100 Greatest Artists of Hard Rock.

2005
Many rock groups participate in Live 8, a series of concerts to raise awareness of extreme poverty in Africa.

1985
Rock stars perform at Live Aid, a benefit concert to raise money to fight Ethiopian famine.

2003
Led Zeppelin's "Stairway to Heaven" is inducted into the Grammy Hall of Fame.

1980
John Lennon of the Beatles is murdered in New York City.

2000s
Aerosmith's album sales reach 140 million worldwide and the group becomes the bestselling American hard rock band of all time.

2007
Billy Joel become the first person to sing the National Anthem before two Super Bowls.

1975
Tommy, the movie, is released.

1975
Time magazine features Bruce Springsteen on its cover as "Rock's New Sensation."

1995
The Rock and Roll Hall of Fame and Museum opens in Cleveland, Ohio.

1970s   1980s   1990s   2000s

1979
Pink Floyd's *The Wall* is released.

1991
Freddie Mercury, lead vocalist of the British rock group Queen, dies of AIDS.

2004
Elton John receives a Kennedy Center Honor.

1979
The first Grammy for Best Rock Vocal Performance by a Duo or Group is awarded to The Eagles.

2004
Rolling Stone Magazine ranks The Beatles #1 of the 100 Greatest Artists of All Time, and Bob Dylan #2.

1986
The Rolling Stones receive a Grammy Lifetime Achievement Award.

1981
MTV goes on the air.

2006
U2 wins five more Grammys, for a total of 22—the most of any rock artist or group.

1986
The first Rock and Roll Hall of Fame induction ceremony is held; Chuck Berry, Little Richard, Ray Charles, Elvis Presley, and James Brown, are among the first inductees.

1981
For Those About to Rock We Salute You by Australian rock band AC/DC becomes the first hard rock album to reach #1 in the U.S.

2006
Bob Dylan, at age 65, releases *Modern Times* which immediately rises to #1 in the U.S.

One word can be used to describe U2 at the 2006 Grammy Awards—domination. The Irish band won every award for which it had been nominated. This photo shows the very happy members of U2 (clockwise from bottom right) Bono, Larry Mullen Jr., the Edge, and Adam Clayton in the pressroom after the awards.

And the Grammy Goes To . . .

February 8, 2006, the forty-eighth annual Grammy Awards: a man wearing a black leather jacket steps onto the stage, U2's lead singer, Bono. He looks relaxed, wearing his famous sunglasses (because of his extremely sensitive eyes). Bono is used to crowds—so he isn't nervous, even though fifteen million people are watching him on television as he gives his acceptance speech:

> **"U2 is not a rock band, really, I don't think so. I think it's like we're a folk band or something—the loudest folk band in the world. But once in a while, there arrives a song, like 'Vertigo,' that makes you want to burn your house to the ground."**

A Thrilling Performance

Suddenly, the houselights go out. White smoke pours onto stage. Strobes flash. "Uno, dos, tres . . . catorce!" Bono shouts out the most famous mistake in Spanish counting. (Instead, of "one, two, three, four," he said "one, two, three . . . fourteen!") The four rock legends slam into the opening of their hit song—made famous by an iPod commercial—"Vertigo."

On Bono's right is the Edge, wearing a stocking cap, as always, and fanning six strings so quickly his hand blurs. On the other side of the stage is Adam Clayton, with short hair and clean-shaven face, fingers flying up and down the neck of his bass guitar. Behind them is Larry Mullen Jr., whose arms flash around the drum set. "Lights go down, it's dark, the jungle is your head. . . ." Bono belts out the opening line of the song, and the audience, most of whom paid more than seven hundred dollars for this show, jump to their feet swaying, screaming, waving.

As "Vertigo" ends, Bono sings a chorus from an old Beatles' song, "She loves you, yeah, yeah, yeah," reminding the audience that today's great artists stand on the shoulders of those before them. Then Edge plays the opening notes of a quieter but more emotional song, "One."

Bono croons into the microphone, "Is it getting better, or do you feel the same?" It seems as if he is speaking one-on-one to each person in the huge concert hall. Suddenly, the audience hears a soaring female voice, as **soul diva** Mary J. Blige steps up behind Bono, microphone in hand. Mary and Bono take turns pouring out their emotions as the words "one," "ein," and "uno" flash on screens behind them. The two singers join hands as they wail out the lyrics, "brothers and sisters, we are one. . . ." As they finish the song, the cheers and applause are like thunder.

Sweeping the Awards

It is a great night for U2. Members of the music industry have nominated the band for five awards: Album of the Year, Song of the Year, Best Rock Song, Best Vocal Performance, and Best Rock Album.

Plenty of other great musicians are also eligible for awards in 2006. For best album, nominee artists include Mariah Carey, the

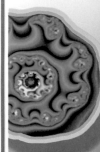

Those attending the 2006 Grammy Awards or who were a part of the worldwide audience were treated to a rare live performance of U2's hit song "One" by Bono and soul singer Mary J. Blige. The powerful duet appears on Mary's 2005 album *The Breakthrough*. Anyone who heard the emotional rendition of the song couldn't help but be moved.

best-selling female vocalist of all time; Sir Paul McCartney, the legendary Beatle; and Kanye West, the critically acclaimed hip-hop artist. In competition with U2 for Song of the Year is a song by Bruce Springsteen. His fans call him "The Boss," and the New Jersey rocker is a long-time friend of U2. For Best Rock Song, nominees include Springsteen's song and "Speed of Sound," Coldplay's chart-topping single.

U2 wasn't at the 2006 Grammy Awards just to pick up their honors. They also gave a rousing performance that brought the crowd to its feet. Complete with a light show, the group's music echoed throughout the Staples Center. The guys had certainly come a long way from their early days in Dublin.

It is a year of amazing music and talent, yet U2 win every award for which they are nominated. Accepting the award for "How to Dismantle an Atomic Bomb," Bono explains the song's title,

"My father Bob was the atomic bomb in question and when he died he set off a reaction in me. . . . I want to thank my father Bob for giving me my voice and my attitude. . . . This is really a big, big night for our band."

Three Chords and the Truth

It is not the first time that U2 has enjoyed walking onto the stage, claiming Grammy Awards. At the 2002 awards, the rockers from Dublin won four Grammys. In one of the band's acceptance speeches that year, Bono said,

> **"It is an extraordinary thing. . . . The promises that your friendship will survive being broke; the Eighties—and maybe 20 years later you will find yourselves at an award ceremony with people you started out with. Wow."**

Indeed, the four members of U2 have a long and amazing career together. They first started playing as teenagers. In the eighties, they exploded onto the **punk** club scene, and over a decade, their fame grew to the point where they could stage some of the greatest concerts in rock history.

At the same time, U2 hopes to make the world better. Bono, especially, is involved with hunger, AIDS, and peace issues. The band's Web site quotes Mahatma Gandhi—"We must become the change we want to see in the world"—and goes on to state:

> **"The music of U2 has always been about heart and mind, body and soul. Down the years the band have successfully thrown a spotlight on the work of key campaigning groups who are trying to make the world a better place."**

In one of their concerts, singing Bob Dylan's song, "All Along the Watchtower," Bono called out, "All I have is this red guitar, three chords, and the truth." With those elements, U2 has made history.

"Drummer seeks musicians to form band." From that note on a high school bulletin board in Dublin, Ireland, one of the most successful and most influential rock groups was born. And the group "has legs." Unlike many bands formed in high school, the four members of U2 have been together for more than thirty years.

2

The Streets of Dublin

Have you tried to start a band with your friends? One of you has a drum set, another a secondhand guitar; you can sing (sort of). So you hang out, make noise, argue . . . and dream of becoming stars. That's the U2 story—except most teen bands break up after a couple of weeks; U2 has stayed together thirty years.

Troubled Youths

In 1976, Adam Clayton, Paul Hewson (Bono), David Evans (the Edge), and Larry Mullen Jr. attended Mount Temple School in Dublin, Ireland. They were normal teen boys—struggling to find their place in the world.

Adam Clayton wasn't too keen on his schoolwork; his favorite thing was his Ibanez-copy bass guitar. He sported a blond afro and glasses, smoked, and wore funky clothes from Afghanistan. He admits he had "no idea" how to play bass.

Paul Hewson (later called Bono) was attractive, energetic, spiritual—and confused. His mother died from a sudden brain hemorrhage in 1974, and he often clashed with his father. Two things that helped him cope—his girlfriend Ali and a religious "revival" that gave him faith in God.

David Evans (later known as the Edge) was a loner at school, but he was a good guitar player. Larry Mullen Jr. was taking drum lessons from a local jazz musician. His father suggested he put a note on the school notice board: "Drummer seeks musicians to form band." Little did he dream this humble notice would call together one of the greatest bands of all time!

Small Beginnings

On Saturday, September 25, 1976, the group met for the first time in the Mullens' kitchen. David Evans came with his brother, Dick, sharing a homemade yellow guitar. Peter Martin came—because he had a guitar and amplifier—with his friend Ivan McCormick—because he knew how to play guitar. Paul Hewson showed up, at the urging of a friend. It was an unremarkable start because, the Edge later recalled, "we were all pretty crap."

They spent most of their time tuning instruments and choosing a name—Feedback, one of the few musical terms they knew. Peter Martin and Ivan McCormick dropped out quickly, but Dick Evans stayed in the band for more than a year, along with David, Larry, Adam, and Paul.

First Concert

Their first performance was a school talent show. They performed Peter Frampton's song "Show Me the Way," because it was easy to play. As the Edge later recalled, when the band got on stage, "suddenly something happened." Bono recalls, "Like you jumped into the sea and discovered you can swim." They weren't very good yet, but they could play—and they loved the applause.

Punk Meets New Wave

Rock music was changing at this time. The boys grew up captivated by the great bands of early rock—such as the Beatles, the Who, the Rolling Stones, and David Bowie. Paul (Bono) learned to play from

The guys who would eventually make up U2 first got together in Larry's kitchen. According to the Edge, there was no indication at that first meeting of the success that would come to the group. Fortunately, for them and for music lovers, they got better.

the *Beatles' Songbook*. At the same time, the torch of rock music was passing hands.

In the early 1970s, rock music focused on fancy techniques; many listeners felt it lost energy and soul. In response, from 1974 through 1976, groups like the Sex Pistols, the Ramones, and Clash brought electronic music back to its roots—loud, fast, and full of attitude. In their first year trying to make music together, U2 played a number of the Ramones' songs.

A movement based on energy and attitude could only stay fresh for a limited time, so after a couple of years, punk music found new direction. When the young men from Dublin began writing their own songs, they were part of the "post-punk" music scene. Two groups were especially important in that movement.

The Boomtown Rats, also from Dublin, managed to gain international fame—proving local boys could hit it big. Their 1978 single "Rat Trap" was the first "New Wave" hit. (Bob Geldof, the Boomtown Rats lead singer, later formed the Live Aid concert and encouraged U2's political involvement.) A group from Manchester England, Joy Division, was one of the most unique and inspiring bands of the era, leading music into the post-punk era and influencing U2.

New Names

The band wasn't the only major influence in Bono's life during this period. His girlfriend Ali was an important steadying influence. Also important were close friends Guggi and Gavin, who had their own group, the Virgin Prunes.

Adam and Paul (Bono), along with Guggi and Gavin, were part of a social group called Lypton Village, which pulled pranks on the streets of Dublin. They were inspired by the British comedy team Monty Python. Members of Lypton Village created their own reality as a protest against the ordinary world.

The members of Lypton Village gave each other new names. Paul Hewson was originally called Steinhegvanhuysenolegbangbangbang. Fortunately for rock fans, they tired of the long name and changed it to Bono, inspired by the name of a hearing-aid store, Bono Vox. It is an appropriate name, since in Latin "bono vox" means "good voice."

David Evans also got a name from the Lypton Village crowd: Inchicore. Can you imagine a concert with Bono announcing; "On

The Boomtown Rats, led by singer Bob Geldof, shown in this photo, were one of the first Irish rock bands to hit it big internationally. Also from Dublin, they showed Bono and the others that such success was possible. In 1985, Bob organized Live Aid, one of the humanitarian efforts that would gain him worldwide fame and respect.

guitar . . . Inchicore!" U2 members changed that to the Edge because, Bono says, "It had something to do with the shape of his head . . . and an insane love he had for walking on the edges of very high walls, bridges, or buildings." Adam Clayton and Larry Mullen Jr. also got special names—Sparky and Jamjar—but those names never stuck, so today fans know them as . . . Adam and Larry.

The Dublin teens had changed their band's name from Feedback to Hype. They realized if they wanted to become any good, they would need more than enthusiasm, so they began rehearsing more. At the same time, they decided to change the group's name *again*.

They came up with a half-dozen names, then chose from that list. None of them were thrilled by the name U2—but no one disliked it, either. Adam thought the name referred to the famous U.S. spy plane; Bono thought of a German submarine (U-boat). Later, they thought of the pun ("you-too"). At the same time, three of the members voted Dick Evans out of the band (they felt it best for David not to vote about his brother).

Tragedy and Trials

In 1978, Larry's mother died in an auto accident. This tragedy brought the members of the band closer together.

The same year, U2 entered a talent contest in Limerick, where one of the judges was an executive with a record company. Bono didn't think they would place in the competition—until the judges announced U2 as the winners. Bono was so excited he accidentally slammed a chair on his father's foot. Their win was an ego boost for the band, but it did not result in the hoped-for recording deal.

U2 knew they needed a good promoter, so they called on Paul McGuinness. McGuinness recalls that when he first saw the band they were pretty ragged, yet he saw that this "baby band" could grow into greatness, so he began to promote them.

The year after high school was difficult for the members of U2, as each had to choose his path: go to college, work . . . or make a go of the band. Bono's father told him, "You've got one year" to make things happen, or "go and get a job."

The same year, U2 was set to tour England, but a promoter failed to come up with promised money. However, the boys' parents raised $500—a large sum at the time—to encourage their dreams of musical success. The band played gigs in London, but they couldn't fill the clubs. Record execs would come, watch, and go away. No record deal materialized.

The band returned to a warm welcome in their hometown because, as the Edge put it, "We were world-famous in Dublin." After a show at the National Stadium there, Nick Stewart, from Island Records, came backstage to offer U2 a record contract—finally.

Boy, and Craziness on Stage

Their first album, *Boy,* released in October 1980, was about childhood and adolescence. The song "I Will Follow" was also released as a single.

Bands need to concentrate on making music—not making business deals. The most successful bands usually have a very good manager or promoter working behind the scenes to get them the best recording contracts and concert gigs. For the guys of U2, that was Paul McGuinness. He recognized the group's potential and set out to make Bono, the Edge, Larry, and Adam a musical powerhouse.

The same year, U2 first toured America, wowing audiences in East Coast punk clubs. Bono was a bundle of energy onstage: dancing, working up a sweat, pulling off his shirt, pouring his heart out. Combined with the Edge's uniquely fast guitar style and the pulsating rhythm from Larry and Adam, the band was a hit.

With money contributed by the guys' parents, U2 set out to tour England. They tried hard, but the group just couldn't get the people out to their concerts. More important, they couldn't find the key that would convince a record company rep to sign them to a deal. It looked as though they would be famous only in their hometown.

Bono's energy, while magnetizing audiences, could also be destructive. At a club in New Haven, Connecticut, Larry's drum set slid on the stage, causing him to mess up. Bono went crazy and threw the drum kit into the audience, then chased after Larry, trying to hit him with the microphone stand. The Edge grabbed Bono's shirt to restrain him, and they got into a fight. Today, Bono is famous for promoting nonviolence, but Bono admits he isn't naturally "peaceful."

Faith

In 1981, U2 released their second and most spiritual album, *October*. The first song, "Gloria," included a Latin chorus of praise to the Almighty. They also did a video of "Gloria," which became popular on MTV.

It was unusual for a popular rock group to sing so much about religion, but those who knew the boys personally were not surprised. In Dublin, Bono, the Edge, and Larry hung around a Christian community called Shalom. On the road, the three gathered in back of the tour bus to read the Bible and pray together. Adam was less spiritually focused at that time, but he appreciated how Christian faith kept the other band members from going crazy over women and drugs—factors that destroyed other bands.

Just before *October* came out, Bono and the Edge faced a crisis of faith. Their fellow believers told them it wasn't God's will for them to play rock music. The boys were torn; they wanted to please God— and they wanted to be the world's best band. At one point, they decided to quit, and they told Paul McGuinness. He replied that they had big commitments and "you're obliged to follow through on them." Fortunately for music lovers around the world, Bono and the Edge agreed. Later, they decided they could serve God with their music.

Years later, their Web site would affirm that the band had

"used their music and their celebrity to highlight and champion countless human rights causes. Nobel Prize winning poet Seamus Heaney says that they have 'sung themselves to where great singing comes from, that place where art and ardency meet in the light of conscience.'"

Most of the guys in U2 have a belief in God. According to Bono, shown in this photo from the early 1980s, God made him a singer because he had a big mouth. But having a big mouth isn't enough to become a musical success. Bono also has talent, which he also feels is a gift from God.

Expanding the Audience

Bono says "extraordinary" things happen when God takes a person's character flaws and turns them into strengths. For example, he admits to having a loud mouth—so, he says, God made him a singer. By 1982, plenty of extraordinary things were happening for U2's members, in both their personal and their professional lives.

The Sweetest Thing

From the moment he first saw her, at age fifteen, Bono knew that Ali—her actual name was Alison Stewart—was the love of his life. She had a calmness that attracted his storm-tossed nature. During the *October* tour, Bono met a married couple he respected, and he told them about Ali. They told him: if you have someone so special, you should go ahead and get married. He took their advice. Bono asked Larry to be his best man, and the wedding took place on August 21, 1982. The newlyweds spent their honeymoon in Jamaica.

Five years later, Bono forgot Ali's birthday because he was so busy recording the *Joshua Tree* album. To make up for this mistake, he wrote the song titled "The Sweetest Thing." In the video of the song, Bono repeatedly says, "I'm sorry." It became a hit, and Ali donated the money from sales of the song to charity.

War and Nonviolence

In 1983, U2 released their third album, *War*. Whereas *Boy* was about childhood and *October* about spirituality, *War* was about politics. The album sold wonderfully. In Britain, the album became the number-one top-seller, knocking Michael Jackson's *Thriller* off the top of the charts.

What made the biggest stir, however, was the song "Sunday, Bloody Sunday." The song is about an incident that happened in 1972, when British soldiers shot and killed twenty-eight Irish protesters in Derry, Northern Ireland. In several interviews, Bono said it is a "positive protest song about things we can't forget." In the song, he asks repeatedly, "How long, how long must we sing this song?" and looks forward to the day when the world can "claim the victory Jesus won" and live together in peace.

Some supporters of the Irish Republican Army (a group that opposes British occupation in Northern Ireland) interpreted the song as a call to violence against Britain. Bono insisted, however, "This is not a rebel song."

The final number on the *War* CD is titled "40." Bono once joked:

"We spent ten minutes writing this song, ten minutes recording it, ten minutes mixing it, ten minutes playing it back, and that's got nothing to do with why it's called '40.' The title comes from the source of the song's lyrics—the fortieth Psalm in the Bible."

The Unforgettable Fire

In 1984, the band produced their fourth album, *The Unforgettable Fire*. Like *War*, it focused on social issues, but in other ways, the album was unique.

"The Unforgettable Fire," an art exhibit at the Peace Museum in Chicago, inspired the album. The exhibition consisted of children's paintings made after atomic bombs hit Hiroshima and Nagasaki. The museum asked U2 for permission to use words from their songs in the display. Workers at the Peace Museum were surprised when all four members of the band showed up to see the art show.

War was a huge seller, and it was also a critical success. Just because an album is a success doesn't mean it isn't without controversy, though. This was true with *War*. Some people thought the song "Sunday, Bloody Sunday" encouraged people in Northern Ireland to fight Britain. According to U2, it was not meant to be a pro-war song.

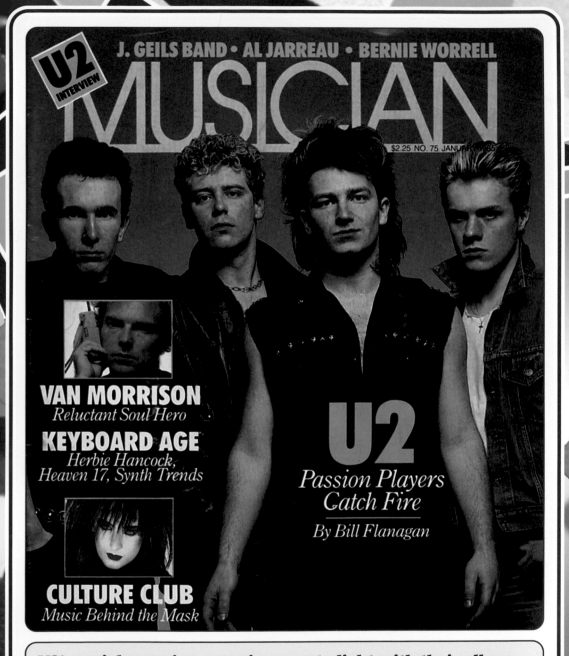

J. GEILS BAND • AL JARREAU • BERNIE WORRELL

MUSICIAN

U2 INTERVIEW

$2.25 NO. 75 JANUARY 1985

VAN MORRISON
Reluctant Soul Hero

KEYBOARD AGE
Herbie Hancock,
Heaven 17, Synth Trends

CULTURE CLUB
Music Behind the Mask

U2
Passion Players
Catch Fire

By Bill Flanagan

U2's social conscience again came to light with their album *Unforgettable Fire*. The album was inspired by post–atomic bombings paintings. Bono, Adam, the Edge, and Larry even visited the exhibition of those paintings at the Peace Museum. Their album also landed them on the cover of *Musician* magazine in 1985.

U2 wanted a fresh sound, so instead of recording in a studio, they chose to cut the tapes in the moody setting of ancient Slane Castle. The band had fun exploring the castle and finding old weapons and outfits. To produce the album, U2 picked Brian Eno, famous for his musical creativity. Eno also worked with Devo, Talking Heads, and David Bowie.

The Unforgettable Fire contains two of U2's best-known songs—"Pride," a **tribute** to Dr. Martin Luther King Jr.'s sacrificial death, and "Bad"—a song about drug addiction. U2 music is always emotional, but this may be their most heart-wrenching album.

Fans and Falls

Bono likes to pull what one critic calls "mischievous stage stunts." U2's front man always finds ways to make physical contact with his audience.

In May 1983, U2 played to their biggest audience yet in Devore, California. Hundreds of lights were attached to metal poles high above the stage where the band performed. The crowd was going wild, and Bono got excited . . . so he started climbing ladders. Speaking to reporter Carter Alan, the Edge recalls, "He ended up climbing four hundred feet to the top of the stage and ceremonially planted the Irish flag and a white flag at the very top. Everyone went bananas! It was incredible!" In his book, *U2: the Road to Pop*, Alan says Bono went up "probably closer to 150 feet"—still a frightening height.

At a huge show in the Los Angeles Sports Arena, Bono wanted to get close to his audience, but the stage was a full story—twenty feet—away from the crowds. As the Edge puts it, sometimes in a show Bono does "really bonkers stuff." He jumped into the crowd. A critic for the *LA Times* said it was the most exciting thing he'd ever seen in a show—as well as the dumbest. Amazingly, the crowd caught Bono, unhurt.

Red Rocks and Rain

Sometimes, the line between huge success and really big failure is incredibly narrow. U2's concert at Red Rocks Amphitheater in Denver, Colorado, June 5, 1983, was a risk that could have been disaster. The band took a quarter of a million dollars—all the money they had earned from shows and records—to film an outdoor concert.

What they didn't plan on for the big show was rain. Lots of rain. Red Rocks is an outdoor concert **venue**; no roof protects the audience, and the day of the show, the clouds poured down buckets. The movie crew said to give up on filming the show. Paul McGuinness, however, was determined that the movie go forward as scheduled.

As the band, their producer, and the film people debated whether to cancel the show, fans—in raincoats and jackets—began pouring into the stadium. What followed was, according to *Rolling Stone* magazine, one of the "50 moments that changed rock 'n' roll."

U2 ran onstage, greeted by a wildly screaming crowed. Bono jumped up and down, prancing, clapping, and belting out lyrics, wearing a thin muscle shirt despite freezing temperatures. Though their fingers were numb from the cold, the Edge and Adam played their hearts out on guitar and bass, while Larry, covered with cold rainwater and sweat, pounded away on the drums. One of the show's directors later told reporter Carter Allen, "It turned out to be an unbelievable performance."

It began with the frenzied excitement of the opening number, "Out of Control." Later came the electrifying moment when Bono danced a jig with a fur-jacketed blond woman from the audience during "11 O'Clock Tick-Tock." The show ended with a memorable rendition of "40," with the Edge playing bass guitar. When the night was over, thousands of fans left the stadium knowing they had seen one of history's great concerts. The film-makers soon converted their footage into a full-length video, titled *Under a Blood Red Sky*, that allowed more people to experience a U2 show.

Live Aid

On July 13, 1985, many of the world's most famous musicians got together to produce an event for a very good cause—the Live Aid Concert, to raise funds for people starving in Ethiopia. Satellites linked live concerts in five different cities around the world, and more than one and a half billion people watched on their television sets. Artists who performed for Live Aid included Mick Jagger, Queen, David Bowie, the Who, Eric Clapton, Led Zeppelin, Bob Dylan, Run D.M.C, the Beach Boys, Madonna, and Elton John. The event raised more than 290 million dollars.

To put it mildly, Bono is a showman. He gets caught up in the music, and sometimes he seems to lose control in his "enthusiasm." And he takes advantage of whatever might catch his attention during a performance. He's climbed metal poles more than 100 feet high, and jumped—unexpectedly— into the crowd. Fortunately, the crowd caught him.

In 1985, Bob Geldof again brought the plight of Ethiopian famine to the attention of the music world—and the fans of rock music. Live Aid brought together music groups in a series of concerts to raise funds. One of the most memorable performances was U2's, with Bono's sudden and unscheduled disappearance into the huge crowd.

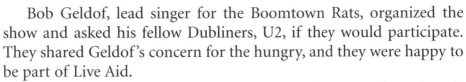

Bob Geldof, lead singer for the Boomtown Rats, organized the show and asked his fellow Dubliners, U2, if they would participate. They shared Geldof's concern for the hungry, and they were happy to be part of Live Aid.

U2 performed at the stage in Wembley Stadium, London. Though they'd played some big shows, the band had never had an opportunity like this one. Can you imagine how it would feel to have more than a billion people watching you on television? You wouldn't want to make any mistakes. So the foursome had a solid plan: they would start playing "Sunday Bloody Sunday," then "Bad," and end their set with "Pride (in the Name of Love)." It was a perfect plan—except it involved the unpredictable Bono.

In the middle of "Bad," Bono disappeared into the crowd in front of the stage, eventually returning and dancing with two young women. In the meantime, the other three frustrated band members played more than five unexpected minutes without their singer. Paul McGuinness stood at the side of the stage, flabbergasted. He thought Bono had completely ruined the event.

But there was more to the story, facts that remained hidden for twenty years. According to *The Sun*:

> **"Kal Khalique was just 15 when Bono saw she was being overwhelmed by the Wembley crowd. The U2 legend leapt off stage and pulled her free—then smooched with her as his band played on. Kal, of Hampstead, North London, said: 'The crowd surged and I was suffocating—then I saw Bono. Security helped him pull me out, then he held me and we danced. My heart was pounding.'"**

Even Bono's craziness was often inspired by compassion. His compassion would lead U2 to even greater feats than this, however.

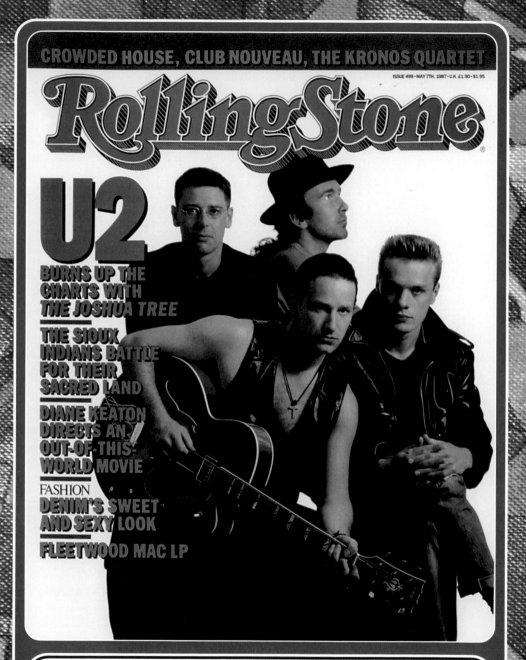

CROWDED HOUSE, CLUB NOUVEAU, THE KRONOS QUARTET

ISSUE 499 · MAY 7TH, 1987 · U.K. £1.90 · $1.95

Rolling Stone

U2

BURNS UP THE CHARTS WITH *THE JOSHUA TREE*

THE SIOUX INDIANS BATTLE FOR THEIR SACRED LAND

DIANE KEATON DIRECTS AN OUT-OF-THIS-WORLD MOVIE

FASHION
DENIM'S SWEET AND SEXY LOOK

FLEETWOOD MAC LP

A band knows that it has found success when it makes the cover of the *Rolling Stone*. *The Joshua Tree* brought U2 to the magazine's cover. The album was inspired by tragedy—and the hope that the Joshua tree symbolizes. The album was a huge success, both critically and commercially as well.

4

Success and Reinvention

"We went . . . to see . . . peasant farmers, who were trapped in the crossfire of this revolution, and we got caught in the crossfire ourselves. I'd never been shot at before." These were Bono's words in *U2 by U2* describing his 1986 tour of Nicaragua. As he traveled throughout Central America, he saw danger, poverty, and wars.

The Joshua Tree

Inspiration for U2's 1987 album *The Joshua Tree* came from the members' recent experiences; 1986 had been an eventful year. Bono's time in Nicaragua led to the song "Bullet the Blue Sky," protesting U.S. military involvement in Central America. Greg Carroll, a New Zealander who worked for the band, died in a motorcycle accident, and grief over his death inspired "One Tree Hill." Phil Lynott, Irish singer for the band Thin Lizzy, died of heroin overdose in 1986, inspiring "Running to Stand Still."

A Joshua tree is a tough cactus that survives in the California desert. *The Joshua Tree* album is also about water and dry places. It speaks of hope in the midst of barren land. Fans and critics loved the new album. U2 won their first Grammy in 1987 for *The Joshua Tree*.

The Tour

Paul McGuinness recalls in *U2 by U2*:

> **"We toured throughout 1987, we were on the cover of *Time* magazine, got Album of the Year at the Grammys, had a number one album and two number one singles in the U.S. It was a dizzying period."**

The Joshua Tree tour was the band's biggest concert series to date—and the craziest. At a show in Washington, D.C., Bono did what the band had long feared: he fell and broke his shoulder. He finished the show, then went straight to a hospital for treatment.

The members of U2 did have some fun on the tour, though. In Indianapolis, the band opening for U2 missed their plane and couldn't make the show, so U2 decided to be their own kicker band; they put on cowboy outfits and wigs and went onstage as "the Dalton Brothers," playing country songs. Fans either ignored or booed the country band, not realizing they were getting an extra performance by U2!

Rattle and Hum

While touring the United States with songs from *The Joshua Tree*, the band hired a film crew to come along and shoot a movie. The project got bigger and bigger to the point where Larry wrote in *U2 by U2*, "It became a monster." Despite troubles making the film, the result, titled *Rattle and Hum*, is a **mesmerizing** road trip across America.

Rattle and Hum celebrates the people and places that contributed to rock, **jazz**, and **blues** music, including rock legend Bob Dylan. Blues man B. B. King plays his beloved guitar Lucille in the movie and adds his soulful voice to the song "When Love Came to Town." The

U2 became movie stars with *Rattle and Hum*, filmed during the group's *Joshua Tree* tour. In this photo, Bono (left) and the Edge (center) discuss a scene for "Redbill Mining Town" with director Neil Jordan (right). In the film, fans see the band paying tribute to some of the icons of jazz and blues.

movie also pays respects to another king—Elvis—as the band visits Graceland, where Larry fulfills a lifetime fantasy by sitting on the King's Harley Davidson.

Staying Fresh

In December 1989, Bono announced, "We've had a great ten years, but we've got to do something else for awhile . . . we can't go on doing this forever." Some fans feared the band might break up. But Bono had in mind a change of direction.

Today's "cool" is tomorrow's "old fashioned." Think how quickly songs, videos, and games become out-of-date. Many rock bands have a few big hits, then spend the rest of their lives playing those same songs. But truly great artists don't get stuck. They reinvent themselves; they change into something no one has seen before.

Achtung Baby

From 1989 to 1991, U2 stepped back from their busy schedule. They used the time to transform themselves. When they came back from their two-year break, their only rule as they made their next album, *Achtung Baby*, was it had to be *different* from anything they'd done before.

U2 was famous for their simple style; on the new album, however, they used **distortion** and **techno beats** to create an entirely different sound. Previously, they had celebrated the musical past of the United Kingdom and United States; this album paid more attention to the rest of Europe, especially Germany.

"One"

Q Magazine declared the song "One" from the *Achtung Baby* album to be "the greatest recorded song of all time." The word *one* can have many meanings, which may be why the song is so great. The lyrics could be a son talking to his father, finding understanding, as the video for the song suggests. The song could also refer to the fact that Berlin—formerly divided into two cities—is now one, after the fall of communism. Much of the profit from the sales of the single "One" went to AIDS charities; maybe "one but not the same" refers to gays and heterosexuals. The layers of meaning make the song a powerful anthem to unity and peace.

Pop Goes the Band

The ZooTV Tour, from 1992 to 1993, was like nothing that fans—or the world—had ever seen. *Q Magazine* called it "the most spectacular rock tour staged by any band." Each show required fifty-two trucks carrying twelve hundred tons of equipment. Enormous video screens flashed clips from television, movies, random videos, and sayings. Cars hung on cables over the audience. The band wanted these concerts to show how video and television influence everything we do and think.

U2 created unique experiences for ZooTV. The song "Mysterious Ways," for example, featured a belly dancer, Morleigh Steinberg (who later became Mrs. The Edge). During the song "Tryin' to Throw Your

Arms Around the World," Bono would dance with a woman from the crowd, spraying both of them with champagne while a video camera projected them onto the huge screen. There was also a **confessional booth** where people recorded personal confessions on camera, which were projected onto television screens during the show.

A 100-foot arch, a 150-foot video screen, and a forty-foot mirrored lemon were prominent players of U2's Popmart Tour in 1997–1998. One stop on the tour was in war-torn Sarajevo. During the concert, fifty thousand fans forgot about their differences. For a while, at least, they all shared the same thing—a love of U2.

The ZooTV Tour also included live television broadcasts from the war zone in Sarajevo. These were a taste of bitter reality in an evening of fun—but the band refused to ignore what was going on in the world.

The Popmart Tour, from 1997 to 1998, was even more amazing. This time, **commercialism** was the theme. Behind the band stood a hundred-foot golden arch, symbolic of McDonald's, and behind that a 150-foot video screen—the largest in the entire world. U2 emerged onto stage from a forty-foot-tall mirrored lemon. Adam recalls in their book:

> **"The lemon was a tremendous toy, it would spin and open up and we'd walk out of it . . . a real show stopper. . . . It literally did stop the show on one occasion, when it failed to open and we had to exit by the emergency escape hatch."**

From beginning to end, Popmart was a mind-blowing, bigger-than-you-could-ever-imagine experience.

One Popmart concert took place in bitterly divided Sarajevo. Fifty thousand fans came to the show, and a reporter wrote afterward, "For two magical hours, the rock band U2 achieved what warriors, politicians and diplomats could not: They united Bosnia." Larry later wrote, "if I had to spend 20 years in the band just to play that show . . . it would have been worthwhile."

Bono and the Devil?

Not everyone loved the ZooTV and Popmart tours. Some fans especially didn't like the roles Bono played during these shows. Sometimes, for instance, he acted a part called "the Fly," wearing wraparound shades and flashy clothing as he acted like a full-of-himself star. Even more disturbing for other fans was Bono's Mr. MacPhisto, a horned character who looked like the devil. Religious fans worried: was Bono serving God or Satan?

They needn't have been concerned. Bono writes, "Mock the devil and he will flee from thee." Everything about the ZooTV and Popmart tours was **parody**. By making fun of the media, businesses—and even the devil—U2 wanted to show the world how foolish these things were. In the 1980s, the band sang about the things they believed in; during the 1990s, they sang about the things they *didn't* believe in.

All That You Can't Leave Behind

If you do anything for too long, it becomes boring. So after Popmart, U2 changed direction yet again. In 2000, they hit the charts with *All That You Can't Leave Behind*, their tenth album on Island Records. This album combined the simplicity of their early sound with the daring new style of more recent songs.

An especially emotional number is "Walk On," which the band dedicated to Aung San Suu Kyi, the imprisoned Asian leader. The

All That You Can't Leave Behind featured "Walk On," a song dedicated to Aung San Suu Kyi, who is in prison in Burma. It is another example of U2's social conscience. But that doesn't mean quality has to be compromised in the name of making a point. The album was another success for the group.

government of Burma told her she could go free, but only if she would leave the country. Determined to settle for nothing but the freedom of her people, Suu Kyi refused and as of January 2007, was still under arrest.

In 2005, it seemed as though everyone had "Vertigo"—at least U2's version. The song, from the album *How to Dismantle an Atomic Bomb*, was even used to sell Apple iPods! The album and supporting tour were huge successes, as people had come to expect from Bono, Adam, Larry, and the Edge.

U2 and 9-11

When people hurt, they often find healing in religion—like going to a funeral for comfort or gathering in a church to pray. Paul McGuinness writes of the band's tour after September 11, 2001, "Those shows were like religious ceremonies." Many fans say that going to U2's Elevation Tour and hearing Bono close the show singing "Hallelujah" was like worship in church (but better). A reviewer from Sonicnet described the band's October 2001 performance in New York's Madison Square Garden:

> **"A performance of 'One' was accompanied by a scrolling list of the September 11 victims on a giant screen at the back of the stage. First came NYPD and FDNY casualties, then the passengers and crew from each of the hijacked flights. And when the band broke into 'Peace on Earth' the names of thousands killed in the World Trade Center began to roll by . . . one could see that the venue was as awash in tears as it was with names."**

"Vertigo"

U2 achieved even greater success with the release of *How to Dismantle an Atomic Bomb*, in November 2004. The album deals with major themes—love, war, peace, and death. Still more success followed in 2005, when U2 was inducted into the Rock and Roll Hall of Fame.

Always looking for something new, U2 promoted their song "Vertigo" on television commercials for Apple's iPod. Some fans were skeptical; was the band selling out? But in fact, U2 turned down the twenty million dollars they could have made for the commercial. They made the commercial, according to Bono, simply because, "The iPod is the most beautiful object in music since the invention of the guitar."

And Now . . .

For three decades, U2 has achieved unbelievable success—and yet they are far from finished. Bono writes, "I'm waking up every day now trying to imagine what we can do next. . . . I think this band's going to get much bigger."

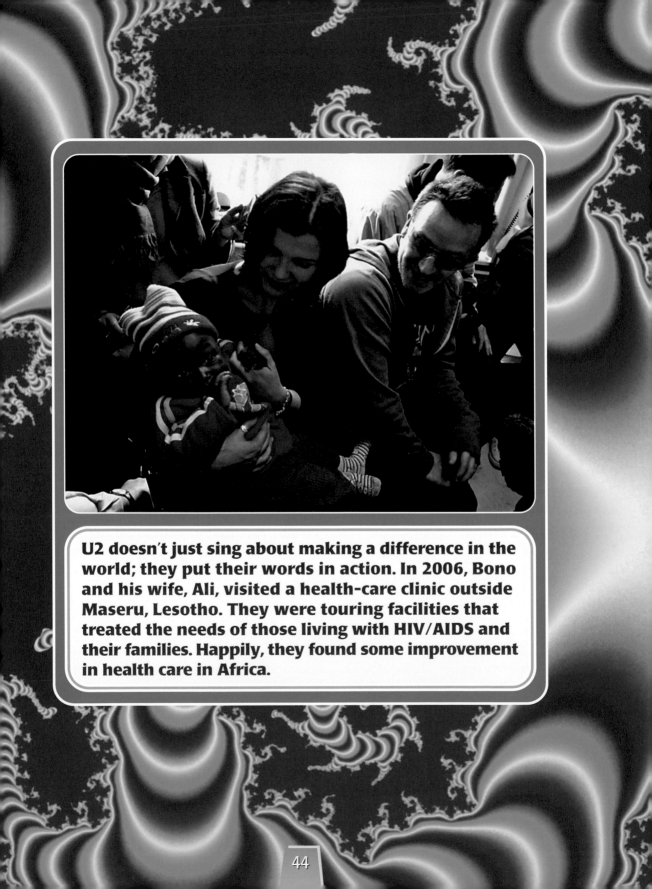

U2 doesn't just sing about making a difference in the world; they put their words in action. In 2006, Bono and his wife, Ali, visited a health-care clinic outside Maseru, Lesotho. They were touring facilities that treated the needs of those living with HIV/AIDS and their families. Happily, they found some improvement in health care in Africa.

5

In the Name of Love

"If you don't take him, he will surely die," a poor Ethiopian father said, holding his starving child before Bono. Bono had to refuse, but the experience changed his life. He writes years later, "if the rage rises up inside of me, it's usually him I'm thinking of." That rage has inspired U2's years of charity work.

Ethiopia

In 1986, World Vision called Bono and asked, "Would you like to see first-hand what's going on in Ethiopia?" World Vision is a Christian organization that provides help where people need food, medicine, or shelter. Bono and Ali agreed to go, and World Vision put them in charge of an orphanage.

Every day in Ethiopia, Bono and Ali saw thousands of people wearing ragged clothes, lined up for food. And every day some of those had to be turned away because there wasn't enough for them. It was a heart-breaking experience, and Bono left with renewed desire to help hungry Africans.

A Conspiracy of Hope

In May of 1986, U2 participated in the Self Aid concert, held in Dublin to benefit Irish unemployed. The fourteen-hour show was the largest held in Ireland.

That same year, U2 played six concerts in the United States to help Amnesty International, a group that urges governments to honor human rights. The Conspiracy of Hope tour was not planned to raise money but to increase awareness of the group's work. U2 is proud to say these shows doubled the membership of Amnesty International.

Global Activist

Today, U2's Bono is famous around the globe, not only as a rock star but also as someone who tries to make the world better. He handles discussions about African politics as easily as he works his guitar and microphone on stage.

He is willing to spend time with anyone who will fight hunger and illness. For instance, Bono met with Pope John Paul II and gave the Catholic leader a pair of his famous sunglasses. Likewise, he met President George W. Bush, flashing a peace sign beside the president. Bono writes:

> **"When I first started going to Washington for meetings on Capitol Hill, I'm sure I looked like a very exotic creature, but eventually they didn't see me, they just saw the argument. And the thing about the pictures of me the rock star with, say, Jesse Helms the politician is—it's really unhip for both of us, you know."**

Live 8

In July 2, 2005, Live Aid organizer Bob Geldof produced an even bigger concert than Live Aid—Live 8. Unlike Live Aid, Live 8 wasn't a fund-raiser; it was an attempt to pressure the Group of Eight (G8)—leaders of the world's most powerful nations—to forgive debts and

In 2005, U2 performed at Live 8. This telethon's goal was to raise awareness of the debt load being carried by some of the world's poorest nations. Held just before a meeting of the G8, the concert encouraged individuals to put pressure on those of the G8 to forgive debts and increase aid to these countries.

increase aid for poorer countries. As Bono said, "We are not looking for charity, we are looking for justice." The event took place just days before the G8 summit meeting in Gleneagles, Scotland. More than a thousand musicians performed on ten stages around the world, broadcast on almost two hundred stations as millions watched.

Almost all the top popular music artists of the world were involved, including the Who, Pink Floyd, Madonna, Mariah Carey, Kanye West, REM, Shakira, Coldplay, Brian Wilson, and—of course—U2. Bono and Paul McCartney opened the London show together. Five days after the Live 8 event, world leaders pledged to double aid to Africa from $25 to $50 billion.

Fighting AIDS and other diseases in Africa is important to Bono. In this photo, Bono (third from left) and Bobby Shriver of DATA (second from left) pose with executives from Carphones Warehouse at the May 2006 launch of Product Red's new phone. The Red Campaign is another way individuals can help make a difference in Africa.

Product RED

Another issue that Bono cares about deeply is help and prevention for AIDS. The numbers are mind numbing: over 22 million people have died from AIDS, and more than 42 million people now live with HIV/AIDS. Three out of four infected people live in sub-Saharan Africa.

At the World Affairs Council in Oregon, Bono spoke out loud and clear on behalf of those who suffer from AIDS and poverty:

"Six million children—and even more adults—die unnecessarily every day of treatable diseases. . . . So put on your boots. Do your part to end stupid

poverty and help eradicate AIDS. This—this is our moon shot.

In January 2006, at the World Economic Forum in Davos, Switzerland, U2's Bono and Bobby Shriver announced Product RED, an economic initiative designed to create a flow of private companies' money to the Global Fund to Fight AIDS, Tuberculosis and Malaria. This was the first time ever that the world's leading companies had made a commitment to channel a portion of their profits from sales of specially designed products to a fund that would support AIDS programs in Africa, with a special focus on women and children— and Bono was one of the driving forces behind the plan. International brands that gave their support to Bono's project included American Express, Converse, Gap, and Giorgio Armani. Each of these companies designed products that would take on the RED mark.

Bobby Shriver, chief executive officer of Product RED, explained how the fund works:

This is a long term initiative designed for sustainability. RED partners expect that they will broaden their own customer base and increase loyalty in a manner that delivers a sustainable revenue stream to both the company and the Global Fund. . . . It's incredible to have the marketing brilliance of these companies behind the AIDS emergency.

Bono was certainly helping to change the world in a very real way. He explained:

RED is a 21st century idea. It's an amazing thing that these companies are doing—lending their creativity and financial firepower to the Global Fund's fight against AIDS in Africa, the greatest health crisis in 600 years. I think doing the RED thing, doing good, will turn out to be good business for them.

A portion of profits from the sale of RED products will support Global Fund-financed programs that impact the lives of women and children affected by HIV/AIDS in Africa. These include programs in countries like Rwanda, which has increased the number of people receiving treatments for HIV/AIDS tenfold.

In October of 2006, Bono joined with talk show host Oprah Winfrey to promote the RED lines of clothing and accessories, including the RED iPod Nano. Bono explained:

> **Now you're buying jeans and T-shirts, and you're paying for 10 women in Africa to get medication for their children with HIV.**

Debt Relief

Bono also campaigns for debt relief for poor nations. Richer nations loan money to poorer nations, expecting repayment; the need to pay that money back makes it harder for struggling countries to help their people. Each year the nations in sub-Saharan Africa, the poorest region of the world, spends $14.5 billion dollars repaying debts to the world's richest countries. Bono has participated in several major efforts to make rich countries release poor countries from debts. These include the Jubilee Campaign, the One Campaign (which Bono founded as a campaign to eradicate poverty), and DATA (Debt, Aids, Trade, and Africa).

Challenging the Church

Many faith-based organizations, including World Vision, are being influenced by Bono's outspoken stance on poverty and AIDS. Rich Stearns, head of World Vision's American branch, has engaged on a cross-country campaign to challenge churches to confront the issue of AIDS; he asks, "Where has the church been while millions have been dying in Africa?" And he often quotes a man he holds up as prophet:

> **What is happening to Africa mocks our pieties, doubts our concern, and questions our commitment to the whole concept [of equality]. Because if we're honest, there's no way we could conclude that such mass death day after day would ever be allowed to happen anywhere else.**

The prophet who said these words is U2's Bono, Stearns reveals, concluding, "We in the faith community must find our voice."

World Vision and the Irish rocker have become close allies. Both were key players in the coalition that last year launched the ONE Campaign, a coalition of advocacy groups and humanitarian organizations devoted to rallying Americans in the fight against global AIDS and poverty. "More and more people are beginning to realize that with

Bono has become a regular participant at political conferences and meetings all over the world. It's no longer an oddity to see the rock star at such events. In 2004, he joined Irish Minister for Development Cooperation and Human Rights Tom Kitt at the EU Development Ministers meeting. They discussed debt reduction, trade, and other development issues pertaining to Africa.

technology and other advances, this can be the generation that ends extreme poverty," said Scott Jackson of World Vision.

Recognized for Doing Good

Because of Bono's charitable work, he has been recognized in a variety of ways from a variety of sources. For example, in 2005, *Time* magazine declared,

> **"For being shrewd about doing good, for rewiring politics and re-engineering justice, for making mercy smarter and hope strategic and then daring the rest of us to follow, Bill and Melinda Gates and Bono are TIME's Persons of the Year."**

On February 2, 2006, Bono was invited to speak at the National Prayer Breakfast. Bono began with these words:

> **"Mr. President, First Lady, King Abdullah, Other heads of State, Members of Congress, distinguished guests . . . please join me in praying that I don't say something we'll all regret. . . . In the Scriptures, poverty is mentioned more than 2,100 times. . . . God . . . is with the poor. . . . And that is what He's calling us to do."**

Bono has even been awarded an honorary British knighthood because of his good works. In December 2006, this press release hit the media:

> **"The British Embassy in Dublin takes great pleasure in announcing that Her Majesty The Queen has appointed Bono to be an honorary Knight Commander of the Most Excellent Order of the British Empire in recognition of his services to the music industry and for his humanitarian work."**

Although the Crown does not give Bono the right to be called "Sir Bono," because the title "Sir" is reserved for citizens of Britain,

Bono has even made an impression on President George W. Bush of the United States. In this photo from February 2006, the president shakes hands with Bono after the rock star's speech at the National Prayer Breakfast. Bono's work on behalf of those most in need has brought him numerous awards and a 2005 nomination for the Nobel Peace Prize.

British Prime Minister Tony Blair said the award is well-deserved for Bono's "remarkable" humanitarian work and for his "outstanding contribution" to music with U2. Blair added in a letter to Bono posted on the prime minister's office Web site:

"I'll leave it to others far more knowledgeable than me to talk about U2's music. All I'll say is that, along with millions of others right across the world, I am a huge fan. But I feel a little more qualified to talk about your personal commitment to tackling global poverty and, in particular, to Africa. I want personally to thank you for the invaluable role you played in the run up to the Gleneagles G8 Summit. Without your personal

Whether trying to change the world through their music or by their actions, U2 has made a difference in the lives of millions of people. Fans inspired by the group's songs and actions take up the causes themselves, or find others meaningful to them. Thanks to Larry, the Edge, Bono, and Adam, the world will be a better place.

contribution, we could not have achieved the results we did. So thank you and I look forward to continuing to work together to maintain momentum on Africa, and ensure leaders around the world meet the promises they have made.**"**

Bono's work for the poor sometimes wears on the rest of U2, who remind him that he does have to spend time practicing and playing. However, he is not the only socially active member of the group. The Edge works with the organization Music Rising, helping replace instruments that New Orleans' musicians lost in Hurricane Katrina.

A Better World

Though they are legendary musicians, in many ways the members of U2 are ordinary people, just like the rest of us. Like anyone else, they enjoy spending time with their friends and family. Bono and Ali have four children: daughters Jordan and Memphis Eve, and sons Elijah Guggi and John Abraham. But in the midst of incredible music and ordinary life, Bono and the rest of the U2 band have found time to make enduring contributions to the world.

Perhaps one of the biggest and most powerful contributions is the stand Bono has taken that calls for us all to get involved. According to one Internet blogger,

"You know how it is when Bono preaches—you leave on fire, determined to help. Because he makes the light bulb go off for you. He makes you believe....""

During U2's downtown San Francisco concert, captured in *Rattle and Hum*, Bono shouts out, "All I've got is a red guitar, three chords, and the truth . . . all I've got is a red guitar, *the rest is up to you!*" With their music, Bono, the Edge, Adam, and Larry inspire us to make the world a better place. The rest is up to us.

1976 Six Dublin teens form the band Feedback; they later change it to Hype.

1978 The group changes its name to U2.

U2 wins a talent contest in Limerick.

1980 Their first album, *Boy*, is released.

1981 *October* is released.

U2 appears on *Tomorrow*, their first U.S. television appearance.

1983 *War* is released

U2 performs at their Red Rocks concert, which is released on video as *Under a Blood Red Sky*.

1984 *Unforgettable Fire* is released.

1985 U2 performs at the Live Aid Concert.

1986 Bono and Ali visit Ethiopia with World Vision.

U2 embarks on the *Conspiracy of Hope* Tour.

1987 *The Joshua Tree* is released, and the group wins a Grammy Award.

The documentary *Rattle and Hum* is released.

U2 becomes only the fourth rock group to be featured on the cover of *Time* magazine, which calls them "Rock's Hottest Ticket."

1991 *Achtung Baby* is released.

1992 U2 embarks on Zoo TV Tour, a multimedia extravaganza.

1997 *Pop* is released.

1998 U2 concludes the Popmart Tour.

2000 *All That You Can't Leave Behind* is released.

2001 U2's Elevation Tour is the top-grossing concert tour in the United States.

2002 U2 plays the Super Bowl half-time show.

2004 *How to Dismantle an Atomic Bomb* is released.

2005 Vertigo Tour is a huge commercial success.

U2 is inducted into the Rock and Roll Hall of Fame in their first year of eligibility.

Bono helps launch the Make Poverty History campaign in Great Britain; it will be called the One Campaign in the United States.

Time magazine names Bono and Bill and Melinda Gates "persons of the year" for their humanitarian efforts.

U2 performs at the Live 8 Concert.

2006 U2 wins five Grammy awards.

Bono and Bobby Shriver launch the (Product) Red campaign.

Albums

1980 *Boy*

1981 *October*

1983 *War*; *Under a Blood Red Sky*

1984 *The Unforgettable Fire*

1987 *The Joshua Tree*

1988 *Rattle and Hum*

1991 *Achtung Baby*

1993 *Zooropa*

1995 *Original Soundtracks No. 1* (as Passengers)

1997 *Pop*

1998 *The Best of 1980–1990*

2000 *All That You Can't Leave Behind*

2002 *The Best of 1990–2000*

2004 *How to Dismantle an Atomic Bomb*; *Live from Boston 1981*;
        The Complete U2; *Unreleased and Rare*

2006 *U2 18 Singles*

Number-One Singles

1987 "With or Without You"
        "I Still Haven't Found What I'm Looking For"

Videos

1983 *Under a Blood Red Sky*

1985 *The Unforgettable Fire Collection*

1988 *Rattle and Hum*

1992 *Achtung Baby*

1994 *ZooTV: Live from Sydney*

1998 *Popmart: Live from Mexico City*

1999 *The Best of 1980–1990*

2001 *Elevation: Live from Boston*

2002 *The Best of 1990–2000*

2003 *U2 Go Home: Live from Slane Castle*

2005 *Vertigo: Live from Chicago*

Book

2006 Bono, The Edge, Adam Clayton, Larry Mullen Jr. *U2 by U2*.
        London: Harper Collins.

Select Awards and Recognition

1988 Grammy Awards: Album of the Year (*The Joshua Tree*), Best Rock Performance by a Duo or Group ("I Still Haven't Found What I'm Looking For"); Sunday Independent/Irish Life Arts Award.

1989 Grammy Awards: Best Rock Performance by a Duo or Group ("Desire"), Best Video Performance, Short Form ("Where the Streets Have No Name").

1992 Grammy Award: Best Rock Group Performance (*Achtung Baby*).

1994 Grammy Award: Best Alternative Album (*Zooropa*).

1995 Grammy Award: Best Music Video—Long Form (*ZooTV: Live from Sydney*); Golden Globe: Best Original Song ("Hold Me, Thrill Me, Kiss Me, Kill Me").

2000 U2 receives the Freedom of Dublin award.

2001 Grammy Awards: Song of the Year, Record of the Year, Best Rock Performance by a Duo or Group with Vocal (all for "Beautiful Day"); *Top of the Pops* Awards: Top Rock Act.

2002 Grammy Awards: Record of the Year ("Walk On"), Pop Performance by a Duo or Group with Vocal ("Stuck in a Moment"), Rock Performance by a Duo or Group with Vocal ("Elevation"), and Best Rock Album (*All That You Can't Leave Behind*); Entertainment Industry Foundation: Bono receives the Heart of Entertainment award for his worldwide charitable work.

2003 Golden Globes: Best Original Song; World Soundtrack Awards (Belgium): Best Original Song; Simon Wiesenthal Center: Bono receives Humanitarian Laureate Award.

2005 Grammy Awards: Best Rock Performance by a Duo or Group with Vocal, Best Rock Song (songwriters award), Best Short Form Music Video (all for "Vertigo"); *Time*: Persons of the Year (Bono with Bill and Melinda Gates).

2006 Grammy Awards: Album of the Year (*How to Dismantle an Atomic Bomb*), Song of the Year ("Sometimes You Can't Make it on Your Own"), Best Rock Performance by a Duo or Group with Vocal ("Sometimes You Can't Make it On Your Own"), Best Rock Song ("City of Blinding Lights"); Bono is knighted for his humanitarian efforts by the British Crown.

Books

Alan, Carter. *U2: The Road to Pop*. Winchester, Mass.: Faber and Faber, 1992.

Assayas, Michka. *Bono: In Conversation*. New York: Riverhead Books, 2005.

Bono, The Edge, Adam Clayton, Larry Mullen Jr. *U2 by U2*. London: Harper Collins, 2006.

Gittens, Ian, and Paul McGuinness. *U2: The Best of Propaganda— 20 Years of The Official U2 Magazine*. New York: Thunder's Mouth Press, 2003.

Scrimgeour, Diana. *U2 Show*. New York: Riverhead Books, 2004.

Stockman, Steve. *Walk On: The Spiritual Journey of U2*. Orlando, Fla.: Relevant Books, 2001.

Web Sites

www.data.org
DATA

www.grammy.com
Grammy Awards Official Site

www.joinred.com
(Product) Red

www.one.org
The One Campaign

www.rockhall.com
Rock and Roll Hall of Fame

www.u2.com
U2 Official Site

www.u2faqs.com
U2 FAQs

blues—A music style that developed from African American folk songs in the early twentieth century and consisting of slow sad songs played over a repeating harmony.

commercialism—Emphasizing the making of money.

confessional booth—A closet-like room where a Catholic goes to confess sins; the priest sits in an adjoining booth to hear the confession.

distortion—The altering of something from its original form into something that becomes unclear or unrecognizable.

diva—A temperamental woman, especially a singer.

jazz—Popular music that originated among African Americans in New Orleans in the late nineteenth century and characterized by distinct rhythms and improvisations.

mesmerizing—Fascinating another person.

parody—A piece of writing or music that deliberately copies another work in a comic way.

punk—A type of loud rock music, often with confrontational lyrics, that characterized a cultural movement of the 1970s.

soul—A style of music that derives from African American popular music with a strong emotional quality related to gospel music and rhythm and blues.

techno beats—Electronic music with strong syncopated rhythms.

tribute—An honor to someone.

venue—Location of an event.

Kenneth McIntosh is a freelance writer, educator, and spiritual guide living in Flagstaff, Arizona. He has written more than three dozen published books. Ken has been a U2 fan since the time when mullets were in style.

Picture Credits

page

2: Newswire Photo Service

8: Hahn/Khayat/Abaca Press

11: Lester Cohen/WireImage

12: Kevin Mazur/WireImage

14: Island Records/Star Photos

17: Island Records/Star Photos

19: Starstock/Photoshot

21: Island Records/Star Photos

22: Mirrorpix

24: Mirrorpix

27: Island Records/NMI

28: New Millennium Images

31: Photo Trend Int'l

32: Mirrorpix

34: New Millennium Images

37: Foto Feature Collection

39: Island Records/NMI

41: BBC/Star Photos

42: Kevin Mazur/WireImage

44: Reuters Photo Archive

47: ZTA/ZOB/WENN

48: UPI Newspictures

51: AFP/NewsFile/Maxwells

53: Owen D.B./Black Star

54: Newswire Photo Service

Front cover: Interscope Records/Star Photos